21 DAY DEVOTIONAL GUIDE

UN-VEILING THE NEW YOU

Becoming un-Stuck

TAMICA JEFFERSON

DEDICATION

I would like to dedicate this book to my

crew, my wonderful family!

My wonderful husband Pastor Carl,

my beloved Daughters Niamiah and Myca.

My favorite Son CJ, You are my Joy and I love

you all immensely!

Table of Contents

Acknowledgments

I would like to share my gratitude and appreciation to all the soldiers in the field who helped to bring this Devotional Guide to Life: My Loving Husband Pastor Carl, thank you for your love, encouragement and supporting me always. I am blessed to be on this journey in life with you I love. Hugs and kisses forever! My Sister Kristina, your love and support are one of the main reasons why I'm rejoicing in this place of newness. My Dearest Mom and Nana Cruz, I Love you and thank you, for the Grace, wisdom and Eldership in my life. Because of Strong Women like you teaching, guiding, and loving me, I am able to stand. Vision Coach Kimberly Springer and the Declare the Morning Win the Day Community, your yes is the backbone to this book. The Father used much of what I learned through my 21 day(s) consecrations and you're coaching to free my mind and Become UN-Stuck!

Thank you Apostle Tanya Tenica and the Truthpreneurs Community! Thank you for your yes and you're gifting to Midwife and help push this baby to be birthed safely and securely. Thank you, for the Un-Veiling process, opportunity and resources; which encouraged me to take the necessary Risk (s) and see this happen. To the Life Change Church Prayer Community (You know who you are). This is our journey together. Thank you for your sacrifice and commitment getting up early each morning and meeting each evening. Faithfully worshiping, praying and experiencing the New the Father has for us. Thank you, Women of God, this is ours!

FOREWARD

"Un-Veiling the NEW YOU" Is not just a 21-day Devotional guide; But its resource can help a person, institution, business, ministry, church, team or family become UN-Stuck. This instruction is a base that will help navigate and walk-through gates of depression, oppression, uncertainty and vulnerability. To uncover a place of peace, rest, guidance and restitution this devotional has something for every stage and perspective. Everyone at some point and place in their lives will or has experienced that stuck place, you will find this authentic conversation with yourself and God captivating as you grapple with the feelings and displacement that comes from being "stuck"

The reality of being "stuck" is something that describes a feeling or place of being paralyzed emotionally. Like the biblical text says about a man for over 38 years who stayed "stuck" in a reality that shaped the way he viewed himself, his circumstance, and how he viewed the world. Only a word and an act of courage changed the way he believed and his narrative suddenly became different.

This is what you will find as you proceed through the chapters of this devotional guide. Real conversation and worship that would change a particular position, pain, perspective and belief. As one writer stated,

"We are set in our ways, bound by our thinking". This is where you will be challenged to rise above, see, and become the "NEW YOU"!

Dr. Maya Angelou, A Prolific writer, poet & author once said, "You may not control all the events that happened to you, but you can decide not to be reduced by them". This is what Pastor Tamica has so effortlessly and succinctly done within this 21-day Devotional Guide. She has helped us to see how what happened to create or cause that place of being "stuck" might not be anything we had control over; but, "Becoming UN-Stuck and Un-Veiling the NEW YOU" is a decision we make and have the power to control.

Carl Jefferson, M. Div, M. Psych
Pastor of Life Change Christian Church
Providence, RI

FOREWARD

Becoming Unstuck has freed my mind from the narrative of negativity I often drowned myself in. As Tamica Jefferson reminds us of the love and provisions God continuously provides for us, we are given a safe space to come face to face with the power of his love and grace.

Tamica holds our hand as we walk through the journey of breaking unhealthy barriers that block us from liberation through the freeing of our minds and the transformation of our thoughts. As a result, we will sing a new song as we move forward to that state of being what God has called for us to be; unapologetically ourselves as we become unstuck to the old us while unveiling the new."

Niamiah Jefferson
Founder of D.I.A Diversity In Action,
Lead Organizer and Motivator,
@ARISE Alliance of Rhode Island,
Southeast Asians for Education.

Preface

HOW TO USE THIS GUIDE

Over these next 21 days, let's be intentional with prayer- worship through song and an active consecration of our minds and thoughts. We'll divide the week in a 3-day view over 7 weeks like this: Monday, Wednesday, Friday (or) Tuesday, Thursday, Saturday. Whichever works well for you. Set a designated meeting time that you will commit to and show up for. This time frame is a time that works well for you. Set your time for 1 hour (yes 1 hour lol).

It helps to divide my hour as such:

15 min- Worship through song

30 min- Prayer regarding what you heard or needs for you, your family, or circumstances

15 min - Scripture Study

BOOM! There's an hour :)

Remember, we are on the journey UN- Veiling the NEW YOU so it's important to show up and follow through. Listed are a few names of The

Lord God, topics to pray, as well as worship songs that I use to help enhance and guide you through this journey. You'll see some of these topics/names/songs repeated at times its purposed that way to stick and go deep within. You can choose whatever worship song that speaks to you. I've listed a few of my favorites found on YouTube that definitely speak more to the direction and intention of that particular day. You can follow Jekalyn Carr using all social media platforms /jekalyncarr, you can also download the TRIBL app or follow-on socials for more live songs and moments with Maverick City Music. (I do not own the rights to the songs listed) Use this book, names of God, worship songs listed, scriptures and prayer; prophetically over your life. Each day speak, mean and believe what you say. READY LET'S GO!! We got this!

PS: Feel free to use this guide over and over again, it takes time for a new habit to stick. I love my 21 days so much; I constantly continue them and I learn something New each time. "New revelation takes place all the time because I'm looking for it" - Tamica Jefferson

INTRODUCTION

Free your Mind

Today is a fresh start to freeing your mind. In Genesis 12:1 the Lord said to Abram, "Leave your country, your people and your father's household and go to the land I will show you". Moving forward often requires new translation in thoughts, actions or deeds. We see in this verse The Father called out Abram with direct instruction. As I meditate on this instruction it's apparent Adoni is leading to interrupt and challenge Abrams ordinary lifestyle and comfortability by telling him to leave. This had to be difficult for Abram to hear and walk out. Being too familiar with thought patterns and actions; although gratifying, can be what keeps you STUCK.

The word of God is living and active and able to instruct, encourage and rebuke all at the same time. We will see the Fathers word alive in us. This instruction, correction and rebuke are all His love and I am grateful for His love. I don't want to assume all is well between you and the Father. If you need to get to know his love or rededicate your life, i.e., getting back on track to freeing your mind in the Lord, say this prayer with me:

Father, thank you for loving me. Thank you for sending The Lord Jesus Christ to die on the cross for my sins. As an act of my will, I renounce and turn away from the practice of sin and wrongdoings in my life. I repent and I ask you Jesus, to be Lord of life and to rule and govern my affairs. I thank you Lord for saving me right where I stand.

If you said this for the first time, WELCOME - Stay connected. You're already UN-Veiling the NEW YOU. If this wasn't your first time saying this prayer and you prayed this again- keep moving forward UN-Veiling the NEW YOU.

Part 1

Egypt

Break-Through

YOU ARE LOVED

Week 1 Day 1

Worship songs: Yahweh, I am Loved - (Maverick City Music | TRIBL Music)

1. Name of God: Jehovah Elohim- The Eternal Creator- Genesis 2:4-25

2. Topic: Focus- Your focus is proclaimed clear to the father

3. Topic: Intention- What is your expectation (speak this, pray out)

4. Topic: Decision- Celebrate and embrace the walk to the new you

Scripture: Hebrews 4:12

Father, the scripture says, the word of God is LIVING and ACTIVE, sharper than any double-edged sword, it penetrates even to dividing soul and spirit, joints and marrow; it judges the thoughts and attitudes of the heart.

What's your intention?

_____

_____

_____

_____

_____

_____

_____

_____

_____

_____

_____

_____

_____

Never Leave, Your Welcome In This Place (Maverick City Music | TRIBL Music)

1. Jehovah Shammah - The Lord is present -Psalms 46, Ezekiel 48:35
2. Father I seek your face- I look to you
3. Guide me
4. I'm Ready

Scripture: Deuteronomy 4:29, 2 Chronicles 14:4

Father, I will seek you Lord with all my heart and all my soul, you are my God. As your word has commanded me to seek your face and to trust your word. Father I declare your words are true, for everyone who asks receives; he who seeks finds and to him who knocks the door will be open. I am asking, seeking and knocking on your door today. Thank you Father the door IS open.

Luke 11:10

What do you see?

_____

_____

_____

_____

_____

_____

_____

_____

_____

_____

_____

_____

_____

_____

You're Bigger, (By Jekalyn Carr "You're Bigger Album")

Major (By Jekalyn Carr, "Changing Your Story" Live Album)

1. El-Hay - The living God - Joshua 3:10, Jeremiah 23:36, Dan 3:26
2. Anoint my ears- quieting our hearts
3. Open my eyes- Interpreting the times
4. Spirit of understanding - to distinguish and discern

Scripture Psalm 20 and Proverbs 2:1-11

Father EL-Hay The Living God, my ears are open and my eyes look for you. Today understanding rests on my heart, distinguishing and discerning what you need for me to know.

What are you discerning?

_____

_____

_____

_____

_____

_____

_____

_____

_____

_____

_____

_____

_____

_____

_____

GETTING RID OF BLOCKAGES

WEEK 2 DAY 1, 2 AND 3

Exodus 3:5-6 "Don't come any closer", God said, "Take off your sandals for the place where you are standing is holy ground. Then he said I AM the God of your father, The God of Abraham, The God of Isaac and The God of Jacob"

How are YOU doing my Friend? Let's keep going this is where we shell off the blockages and hindrances. This is where we take our sandals off. Your shoes serve as a protective barrier between you and the surface. The father speaks to Moses and tells him to take off your barriers. Any blockage that is in the way past or present. The place where you are standing is holy ground. The father is saying I want to touch you and I want you to touch me; so, rid yourself of any protective blockages that will keep this from taking place.

What(s) in the way?

_____

_____

_____

_____

_____

_____

_____

_____

_____

_____

_____

_____

_____

_____

WRITING THE LETTER(S)

Writing a letter may seem difficult or like a mundane chore. Trust me, the freedom that comes with writing it out, with the intention of letting go is very rewarding. When the Father instructed me to write my letters, I was nervous because of the feelings of hurt and pain they would bring up for me. I knew in order to move past the hurts I needed to acknowledge them. After all, I was playing the song of defeat in my heart and my thoughts. It affected my moods and my relationship with people and the lens I saw them through.

Keeping in mind this exercise is to RELEASE the offense and let it go. I'm not saying the offense isn't important enough to rectify with the other parties. I'm saying to move forward and have the father's peace; this is a sure way to renew your mind to be free and not in bondage any longer. In Luke 23:34 when Jesus was on the cross, he said: "Father forgive them, for they do not know what they are doing"

Write it out, to let it go:

_____

_____

_____

_____

_____

_____

_____

_____

_____

_____

_____

_____

_____

_____

DEBT FREE

To forgive a debt free is to acknowledge there is a debt, something owed. But, we are choosing to wipe the debt clean. It's not that we aren't acknowledging the offense whatever it is; but instead, it's saying Yes, I was hurt or offended by .... And even though you may or may not have meant to hurt me, I choose to no longer hold this against you. I choose to let you go in Jesus' name.

This is a very powerful act of reclaiming the NEW YOU. Through the thoughts and the pain, you are choosing to forgive the individual(s) and allow yourself to be nailed to the cross for the sake of healing.

These letters may be written to people who are living or may not be here any longer. The purpose of the notes is to acknowledge your hurt... and get it out... Write it out and let it go, allow yourself to be free there. My first letter was to myself. Yep, I had to forgive myself for some things first. Then the Holy Spirit helped me where and who to write to next. After writing these letters, you tear them up or throw them away. I put mine on my charcoal grill and had it go up in smoke. This was my act never to be remembered or reminded again. Walking in freedom the NEW YOU. It's done.

ABBA Father, Today I choose to be DEBT FREE, I choose not to hold any account against myself or anyone else. I choose to live clear, to think clearly and be clear. I take off any blockages that will hinder my freedom in you. I am a NEW creation in you.

Debt-free Living/ This is what I Choose:

_____

_____

_____

_____

_____

_____

_____

_____

_____

_____

PART 2

WILDERNESS

=

DEVELOPING

IT'S DONE, I'M MOVING FORWARD

Week 3

Isaiah 42: 8-10 "I AM the Lord that is my name! I will not give my glory to another or my praise to idols. See, the former things have taken place and new things I declare; before they spring into being I announce them to you."

Wilderness = Developing

Many of us see the wilderness and think of it as a bad experience, dry season or a hard time. If we take a closer look at the development in the wilderness, we will see this is the place the father reveals himself directly to us. The wilderness experience is where we see Adonai is Adonai, His hand and miracles. This is where our eyes are keen to see the impossible become possible.

This place is noted in the scriptures for water coming from rocks, fresh food daily (manna) from heaven, promises and establishment and many more miracles. This place is the activation of your personal salvation, power and redemption! Beautiful, beautiful it's beautiful, the wilderness is a necessary experience to help you to forget the past (Egypt) and all the time you spent there. You have to forget your Egypt, leave it behind; because you can't take Egypt into Cannon. So, develop, grow and remain teachable in the wonderful wilderness. You're becoming the NEW YOU.

Changing your Story, You've Been Restored

(By Jekalyn Carr, Changing Your Story Live Album)

1. Jehovah Goelekh- The Lord Thy Redeemer Isaiah 49:26, 60:16

2. Deliverance FROM Egypt

3. Development IN Wilderness

4. Destiny TO Cannon

Scripture: Philippians 4:6-7, Isaiah 26:3-4

ABBA Father, I praise you and thank you for I am Blessed and Loved by you. I have been restored.

What is it you're looking to learn?

_____

_____

_____

_____

_____

_____

_____

_____

_____

_____

_____

_____

_____

_____

_____

Promises (Maverick City Music | TRIBL Music)

1. Jehovah Nissi - The Lord our Banner Exodus 17:15

2. Moving forward

3. Development in the Wilderness

4. Discover ABBA in the Present

Scripture: Philippians 3:13

Abba Father, I take hold and open my heart to move forward in you, physically, emotionally, mentally, spiritually and economically. Today I see you abba in my present and am grateful.

What are you moving forward towards?

_____

_____

_____

_____

_____

_____

_____

_____

_____

_____

_____

_____

_____

_____

Fill The Room, Holy Ghost, Promise (Maverick City Music | TRIBL Music)

1. Jehovah Rohi- The Lord is My Shepherd - Psalm 23:1

(The Fathers Perspective)

2. How the Father- thinks about it

3. How the Father - Feels about it

4. What the Father - Expects from me

Scripture: Joshua 1:2-9

Lord, open my eyes to see you. That I may understand your thoughts about me and know how to grow in that place, so I can flourish in my assignment(s).

How does the father see you in this new place?

_____

_____

_____

_____

_____

_____

_____

_____

_____

_____

_____

_____

_____

_____

_____

_____

WHAT ARE YOU THINKING

Week 4 Day 1

You're Welcome In This Place, Man Of Your Word (Maverick City Music | TRIBL Music)

1. Jehovah EL- Elyon - The Lord Most High - PS 7:17, 47:2, 97:9
2. Cancelling old Thoughts (controlling thoughts)
3. New Thoughts
4. Freedom in taking NO Thought

Scripture: Isaiah 55:6-13, 2 Corith 10:3-5

Father, today I take captive every negative thought that doesn't come from you. Your ways are not my ways neither are your thoughts my thoughts. Today I put on the helmet of salvation. Renewing every thought that doesn't work for me, I submit it to you. I walk in the newness and freedom of Christ Jesus. You are the truth and whom the Son sets free is free indeed!

What thoughts are you destroying forever?

_____

_____

_____

_____

_____

_____

_____

_____

_____

_____

_____

_____

_____

_____

Jireh | (Elevation Worship & Maverick City Music),

My Heart Your Home (Maverick City Music |TRIBL Music)

1. Jehovah Shalom- The Lord our Peace Jude 6:24

2. Leaning in

3. Emotional Peace

4. Emotional Freedom

Scripture: 2 Corinthians 10:3-5, Ephesians 6:10-12, 1John 5:4-5

Amen Father! I'm determined to embrace - envelop your peace. I am leaning in, taking hold of my emotional peace. I have the power to think NEW thoughts. I control my thoughts and I choose to think, feel and express myself in your peace Shalom. You are Peace and in you, there is freedom and rest.

How will you take hold of God's REST?

_____

_____

_____

_____

_____

_____

_____

_____

_____

_____

_____

_____

_____

Changing Your Story, Restored (By Jekalen Carr "Changing Your Story Live" Album)

1. El Rai - God sees me - Gen 16:13
2. Changing your Story
3. Rename It
4. Believe and Reshape It

Scripture: Isaiah 55:6-13, Mark 7:15

Father, this mindset is making me NEW. You are indeed Changing my memoir. I'm renaming- reshaping every thought. From death to life, bondage to deliverance. From hated to loved, rejected to received. From failure to achieve, lonely to beloved and from deficiency to plenty. Amen.

What are you renaming?

_____

_____

_____

_____

_____

_____

_____

_____

_____

_____

_____

_____

_____

_____

SING A NEW SONG

WEEK 5

Isaiah 42:10 Sing to the Lord a NEW song, His praise from the ends of the earth, you who go down to the sea, and all that is in it, you Islands, and all who live in them.

Who does the Father say you are? What is heaven saying about you? What are the angels waiting to hear you say? What instruction are you communicating? When ABBA sees you, what is he saying regarding you? While you're answering these questions, it's important to remember Isaiah 55:8 "For my thoughts are not your thoughts, neither are your ways my ways," declares the Lord.

Singing a NEW song is seeing the best version of yourself. Innovative, progressive, creative, not restrictive. Blessed beyond measure. When ABBA sees you, what is He saying regarding you?

Who are you?

_____

_____

_____

_____

_____

_____

_____

_____

_____

_____

_____

_____

_____

_____

_____

_____

_____

It Has Been Established (By Jekalyn Carr, One Nation under God Album)

1. Jehovah Jireh -Gen 22:8-14
2. Perfect Timing
3. You're Covered
4. Glory for This

Scripture: Joshua 1:6-9

Amen Father, I'M OK!! Mines is the kingdom of God. I will be comforted, I will inherit the earth, I will be shown mercy, I will be filled, I will see you, Lord, in the Land of the living, I am called a (son or daughter) of the Most High God. I am the light of the earth because the Lord dwells within me. I am a city set on a hill that cannot be hidden. Worry is not within me; doubt has no place. You, Lord, haven't given me a spirit of fear. I am important to you and as I knock, the door will be open. Heaven IS open to me.

What do you have glory for?

_____

_____

_____

_____

_____

_____

_____

_____

_____

_____

_____

_____

_____

_____

Connected To You (By Jekalyn Carr, "Changing Your Story" Album)

1. Jehovah Eloheka - The Lord Thy God - Exodus 20:2, 5, 7
2. ABBA First
3. Exclusivity Clause
4. No Competing Loyalties

Scripture: Exodus 20:2-6, John 6:35

Father, exclusive honor I give to you, thank you for exclusive rights, exclusive love, exclusive time, exclusive favor, exclusive teaching, exclusive rebuke, exclusive power. Father, when you see me, you see the Blood Covenant through your Son the Lord Jesus the Christ.

In what way are you EXCLUSIVE to God?

Wait On You (Maverick City Music & Elevation Worship - Old Church Basement Album)

1. Jehovah Tsidkeenu - The Lord our righteousness Jeremiah 23:16
2. I'll Wait on You Lord
3. Instruction
4. UN-Veiling

Scripture: 2 Corinthians 3:15-18

My Lord, I'm Blessed, UN- Veiled and Free Amen!

How are you UN-Veiled?

_____

_____

_____

_____

_____

_____

_____

_____

_____

_____

_____

_____

_____

_____

_____

PART 3

TAKING

HOLD OF

CANAAN

SEE, HEAR, SMELL

WEEK 6

Our senses; by which our body perceives as external stimulus; such as sight, hearing and smell taste and touch provides awareness, perception and sensibility. These neural pathways are responsible for processing information to your brain.

This week we will use our senses to expand and concentrate, specifically to see the Father, to Hear the Father and Smell Him. Come now, gathering this information will guarantee keys and abundant access throughout the scriptures activating faith catapulting that greatness that's already in you.

What are your senses telling you?

_____

_____

_____

_____

_____

_____

_____

_____

_____

_____

_____

_____

_____

_____

Goodness of God, Ways for me (Maverick City Music | TRIBL Music)

1. EL Rai - God sees me - Gen 16:13

2. Eyes to see you - (seeing you differently)

3. Peace - Choose to embrace-Put on

4. Show Up- Assignment

Scripture: Gen 16:13, Job 42:5, John 14: 9-21

Father, thank you for seeing me. I have seen your hand, your strong mighty arm that makes ways in the wilderness. Anoint my eyes to see you in all NEW Ways.

What do you see?

_____

_____

_____

_____

_____

_____

_____

_____

_____

_____

_____

_____

_____

_____

_____

_____

_____

Goodness of God, Yes & Amen (Maverick City Music | TRIBL Music)

Major - Jekalyn Carr (By Jekalyn Carr "Changing Your Story" Album)

1. Jehovah Eloheenu - The Lord our God - Psalm 99:5, 8, 9

2. Ears to hear (Hearing you differently)

3. Reveal - Make plain your truth

4. Accumulation - Gathering of information

Scripture: Ezekiel 33:7, 37:4, Matthew 11:15, Job 42:4-5

Thank you Lord, for the assignment that is ready for me. My ears are open ready to hear, Speak Lord your servant is listening!!

What do you hear?

_____

_____

_____

_____

_____

_____

_____

_____

_____

_____

_____

_____

_____

_____

WEEK 6 DAY 3

Never Leave, Isaiah Song (Maverick City Music | TRIBL Music)

1. Jehovah Elohim - The Eternal Creator - Gen 2: 4-25
2. Smell you Lord -Perceiving, Detecting, Noticing
3. To Know You (Understand you differently)
4. Making room for you

Scripture 1 Kings 3:12, Proverbs 1:5, 14:6, 15:14 Philippians 1:9-10

Father, I will smell you so that I may know you, really know you. I open my nostrils to smell your sweet aroma. The aroma of your spirit that gives me rest in you; because you are with me.

How are you detecting the Spirit of The Lord?

_____

_____

_____

_____

_____

_____

_____

_____

_____

_____

_____

_____

_____

_____

_____

OH TASTE

WEEK 7

Taste and see that the Lord is good, Blessed is the man who takes refuge in Him. How sweet are your promises to my taste, sweeter than honey to my mouth! Eat, honey, my son, for it is good; honey from the comb is sweet to your taste. Know also that wisdom is sweet to your soul; if you find it, there is a future hope for you, and your hope will not be cut off. Therefore, rid yourselves of all malice and all deceit, hypocrisy, envy, and slander of every kind. Like newborn babies, crave pure spiritual milk, so that by it you may grow up in your salvation, now that you have tasted that the Lord is good.

Psalm 34:8, 119:103, Proverbs 24:13-14, 1 Peter 2:1-3

Awesome, Awesome, Awe-Some! This is the week we gird our waistband. Tie it up around your waist. Look with eager expectation for the arrival of our Lord! Get ready as you taste, you will see the glory of the Lord in the Land of the Living.

What is your Taste-timony?

_____

_____

_____

_____

_____

_____

_____

_____

_____

_____

_____

_____

_____

_____

_____

Testify, Never Leave (Maverick City Music | TRIBL Music)

1. Jehovah Shammah - The Lord is Present - Psalm 46
2. I AM - With you
3. Taste - (Him Differently)
4. Open Heaven

Scripture: John 1:1-5, Deuteronomy 8:18, Isaiah 41:10

Father, my mouth is open... to proclaim, to declare, to praise, to taste and to testify of your goodness; because you are with me!

Taste-tify!!

_____

_____

_____

_____

_____

_____

_____

_____

_____

_____

_____

_____

_____

_____

_____

_____

_____

WEEK 7 DAY 2

Man of Your Word, Wait on You (Maverick City Music | TRIBL Music)

1. Jehovah Eloheka - The Lord Thy God Exodus 20:2,5,7
2. Take A Risk
3. Answered Prayers
4. It is Finished- The Done Place

Scripture: Isaiah 41:13

Father, I will go, I will do, it's done. I have seen and I will taste it, it is finished!

Embrace the RISK? What's your RISK?

_____

_____

_____

_____

_____

_____

_____

_____

_____

_____

_____

_____

_____

_____

_____

Ways for Me, Isaiah Song (Maverick City Music | TRIBL Music)

1. EL Hay - The Living God -Joshua 3:10

2. Living Water

3. New Perspective

4. You Are Enough

Scripture: Gen 2:10-15, John 4:10, Rev 22:1-3

Father, you're making ways for me in every area, so let it be!

What's your NEW Perspective?

_____

_____

_____

_____

_____

_____

_____

_____

_____

_____

_____

_____

_____

_____

_____

LIVING WATER

Great Job, I'm so happy, you must feel really good! You have accumulated the information. You are assimilating, taking on this truth, doing the work to position for the next level. Now it's time to activate that faith and take a risk. In Genesis 2:4-6, 10-15, when the Father created the heavens and earth it was the stream of water in vs 6 that formed man. (Living Water) In vs 10-15, we see the provisions, the richness of His goodness as the river flows throughout the garden of life. This river has four headstreams, which extend throughout the land. The scripture says gold, onyx, aromatic resin and all the goodness needed to supply for the land flowed through the river. Jesus said in a loud voice John 7:37-38, "Whoever believes in me, as the scripture has said streams of living water WILL flow from within him"

Jesus said, "If a man is thirsty..." LISTEN!! I am Thirsty, are you? After the work we've done letting go of the past, growing, seeing and thinking differently it's time to flow in that done place. In John 6:5-6, Jesus says to the disciples in vs 5 when he saw a great crowd coming to Him, "Where shall we buy bread for these people to eat?" Vs 6 He asked only to TEST them for He ALREADY had in mind what he was going to do. Jesus already had in mind what he was going to do before the miracle happened where he fed the people. In vs 10+12 says there were about 5,000 men vs 12 it says they all had enough to eat, so much so they gathered the extra pieces that were left over and he instructed them "let nothing be wasted". (My Lord)

This next *New* start in your *New* beginning is to take a risk. Take the necessary risks to authenticate yourself: *New* level, *New* perspective, *New* mind, *New* feelings, *New* faith and *New* territory. Taking the risks help, you embrace your *New*.

Isaiah 43:1-3 says fear NOT. There's something about resting in the Lord. Trusting fear is to believe there is danger in which someone or something is likely to cause pain or a threat. I'm talking about impure fear. The father hasn't given us a spirit of fear, but of power, love and of self - discipline 2nd Timothy 1:7. In 1John 4:18 "There is NO fear in love. But perfect love drives out fear because fear has to do with punishment. The man who fears is not made perfect in love."

My husband and I have a fellow congregant whose mother weren't doing too well in the Hospital. The doctors and some family members grew impatient with the healing turnaround time. The ventilator was helping her breathe, which made the process prolonged and more difficult to bear. No one wants to see their loved one hurting and in so much pain. So, the thought was to remove the ventilator and allow her to transition naturally and peacefully. It was Monday this decision was to take place on the upcoming Wednesday. The situation and circumstance looked grim, so we were preparing our minds to say its ok Father, thank you for her life. I went into prayer as I normally would, you know in "Faith" so I thought.

As I began to open my mouth, The Father stopped me in my tracks while the words were forming in my mouth and he said, "You know my Name"! In a question yet in a declaring form. I said, "Yes, Lord I do," He said, "You know who I AM"! I said, "Yes, Father I do," He said "Then, don't come to me like this- Don't come to my throne in DOUBT," He said, "Go back out and come again"! I said "Yes Lord." Mind you, at the start I didn't come to the Father any different from the way of which I'm used to coming in to pray. He said, "You can't pray (*for*) anything in DOUBT, it's impossible!" I said, "Yes Lord." At that moment, I changed my heart, my thoughts and the way my words were expressed regarding the healing that needed to take place.

As I changed the expression of my words in prayer, heaven began to move which made room for the miracle to take place. The risk was to believe He rewards those who earnestly seek Him. When they removed the ventilator, she started breathing on her own. This stunned the doctors, family and friends.

*Praying (**for**) something without Doubt?*

_____

_____

_____

_____

_____

_____

_____

_____

_____

_____

_____

_____

_____

_____

_____

_____

You can pray for positive powerful words; but it's the How in the expression that casts doubt. Hebrew 11:6 And without faith it is impossible to please God because anyone who <u>COMES</u> to Him <u>MUST</u> believe that He exists and that He <u>REWARDS</u> those who earnestly seek Him!

Most people don't realize the doubt that's deep within. We know God exists and we love Him too. It's the faint question that raises reservations in our hearts. Will God do this for me? Does he even hear my prayers? What if he doesn't? Will I look stupid to others? I know He exists, but do I believe (this) can happen? Am I looking forward to this happening, even though these are words I should just say and pray? Who am I kidding?

This is that vulnerable risky place called faith. This right here is what most believers war between these two (faith and doubt) on their best day. "For out of the overflow of the heart the mouth speaks" Matthew 12:34. So it's OK to go out and come in again, this time fixing your words to line up with Him. It's not what you say it's how you say it, so say it like you know WHO He is and knowing WHO you are without any DOUBT.

I'm reminded of the movie "The Matrix", there is a character named Neo. Neo is challenged with thinking differently, seeing differently, believing differently out of the box. The box in this story is the matrix. The restrictions, what we tell ourselves to believe. Out of the box in the organic view is the type of thinking it takes to take the risks. The New you require New challenges and experiences. New networks, New opportunities. Faith is unseen so radically. Trusting the Father is with you, really with you, and that you are not alone. You are enough just as you are, you can learn as you go. You'll grow wings as you fly.

Isaiah 43:1-3 says God has called you by name, you are His. When you pass through (rivers), you will not drown. When you walk through (fire), even though it may be hard at times - pressing through, you will not be consumed. He is the Holy One and He has you. John 6 says if you believe in Jesus, you will have life. Take the time to read John 6 Jesus speaks about it all from the beginning to the end. He already has you covered and taken care of. Pray, listen, do. Then take the Risk! Believe and go, it's Your New season - You Got This!!